ROT AND DECAY

A Story of Death, Scavengers, and Recycling

Sarah Levete

Rourke
Publishing LLC
Vero Beach, Florida 32964

www.rourkepublishing.com

PHOTO CREDITS: p. 22: Alexsander Bolbot/ istockphoto.com; p. 40: The Bridgeman Art
Library/Getty Images; p. 34: British Polythene Industries plc; p. 6: Alexander Chelmodeev/
istockphoto.com; pp. 9, 23, 43: Corbis; p. 26: Andriy Doriy/istockphoto.com; p. 25: Nicole
Duplaix/Getty Images; p. 27: Chris Fairclough; pp. 10, 14: Chris Fairclough/CFWImages.com;
p. 5: Rebecca Grabill/istockphoto.com; pp. 7, 18, 20, 28: istockphoto.com; p. 37: Ben
Luxmoore/Arcaid/Corbis; p. 4: Bradley Mason/istockphoto.com; p. 17: Peter Miller/
istockphoto.com; p. 19: Mark Moffett/Minden Pictures/FLPA; p. 39: NASA; p. 35: Edward
Parker/EASI-Images/CFWImages.com; p. 16: Michael Pettigrew/istockphoto.com; p. 21:
Photodisc; p. 31: Amanda Rohde/istockphoto.com; p. 29: Brendan de Suza/istockphoto.com;
p. 33: Svensk Biogas; p. 32: Jacob Taposchaner/Getty Images; p. 24: Harold Tjostheim/
istockphoto.com; p. 41: Emrah Turudu/ istockphoto.com; p. 42: Beverley Vycital/
istockphoto.com; p. 12: Nathan Watkins/ istockphoto.com; p. 13: Bert van Wijk/
istockphoto.com.

Cover picture shows a fly feeding on decaying fruit [istockphoto.com].

Produced for Rourke Publishing by Discovery Books
Editors: Geoff Barker, Amy Bauman, Rebecca Hunter
Designer: Ian Winton
Cover designer: Keith Williams
Illustrator: Stefan Chabluk
Photo researcher: Rachel Tisdale

Library of Congress Cataloging-in-Publication Data

Levete, Sarah.
  Rot and decay : decomposing and recycling / Sarah Levete.
      p. cm. -- (Let's explore science)
   ISBN 978-1-60044-602-3
  1. Biodegradation--Juvenile literature. 2. Recycling (Waste, etc.)--Juvenile literature. I.
Title.
  QH530.5.L48 2008
  577'.16--dc22
                              2007020410

Printed in the USA

CONTENTS

CHAPTER ONE

LIFE AND DEATH

Look around in a park or a garden. Some plants will be growing. Others will be dying and beginning to decay, or rot. This means they break down into small parts, or **decompose**. The same process happens to animals. They are born, they grow, and they die and decay. It just is not always as easy to see.

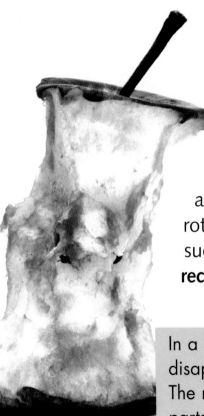

Many manufactured (human-made) objects, such as plastic toys, are made of materials that do not rot. These objects and other materials, such as the metal in a can, may be **recycled** and turned into something else.

In a few weeks, this apple core will have disappeared. Insects will eat some of it. The rest will be broken down into tiny parts. These will soak back into the soil.

Natural materials such as leaves rot back into the soil. Manufactured objects such as this polystyrene cup take much longer to break up.

This book explains the process of decay. It looks at how nature cleans up the remains of dead plants and animals and what it does with those remains. But we can't talk about decay in the natural world alone. This book also tells you what happens to manufactured objects when they are no longer useful.

A Natural Cycle

Everything that lives eventually dies. Some animals and plants die from age or disease. Others are eaten by other animals. Nature has an army of helpers to clean up the remains.

Make Way

The lives of many living things depend upon the death of others. Imagine if animals and plants did not die. There would not be enough space or food for new plants and animals to grow. The death of plants and animals makes it possible for new lives to thrive.

Older plants and trees die and make way for new growth, such as this young oak tree.

Flies spread disease but their young, called maggots, feed on the rotting flesh of plants and animals.

Nature's Recyclers

Nature has been recycling for millions of years. The remains of animals and plants rot and decay is a process called decomposition. Plants and animals called decomposers eat away at natural waste. Natural waste comes from anything that was once alive. It is also called **organic matter**. As decomposers break up the waste, they release **chemicals** into the **environment**. These chemicals provide energy and food, called **nutrients**, for other plants and animals.

A Balancing Act

An **ecosystem** is the balance between a community of animals and plants and its environment. Decomposition is part of that balance. Through decomposition, nature is constantly recycling natural waste such as rotten leaves. So, next time you walk on a pile of damp leaves, remember it's nature at work!

The Food Chain

A **food chain** also helps balance the ecosystem. A food chain transfers food energy from one animal or plant to another. When an animal eats something, it forms part of a food chain. For instance, green plants make food from sunlight. This process is called photosynthesis.

Plants absorb the gas carbon dioxide and change it to sugar. They give off the gas oxygen as a waste product. Plant-eating animals feed on the plants and take in the energy made by plants. This passes to the next animal who eats the plant-eating animal, and so on.

THE FOOD CHAIN

Shrimp eat pond weed, frogs eat shrimp, and fish eat frogs. This is an example of a food chain in a pond.

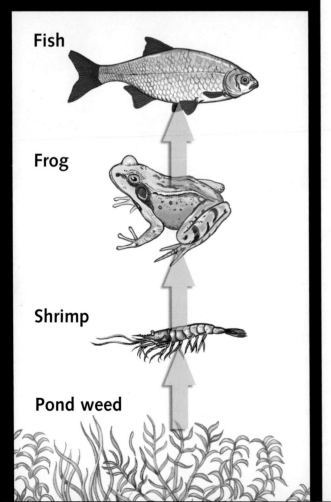

Fish

Frog

Shrimp

Pond weed

These towering redwood trees form part of the complex balance of animals and plants called the ecosystem.

Even decomposers are part of the chain. When decomposers attack dead plants and animals, they too take in some of this food. The rest is broken into nutrients, like nitrogen. These soak back into the soil. Meanwhile, the gas carbon dioxide is released into the atmosphere. The nutrients released help other plants grow and provide food for other animals.

Rotting to Breathe

Earth cannot survive without oxygen and carbon dioxide. The flow of these gases depends upon decomposers. Decomposers break down dead matter. They change carbon stored in the waste into carbon dioxide. The gas is released into the atmosphere along with oxygen which is produced as decomposers work.

CHAPTER TWO

ALL ABOUT GARBAGE

A potato chip bag is useful for holding potato chips. Once you eat the chips, you will throw away the bag. The things you throw away are garbage.

Types of Garbage

Most garbage is solid. This includes things such as plastic containers or the remains of a sandwich. Garbage can also be a liquid, such as oil. Sometimes garbage may even be a gas.

Garbage left lying around attracts disease-carrying animals such as rats.

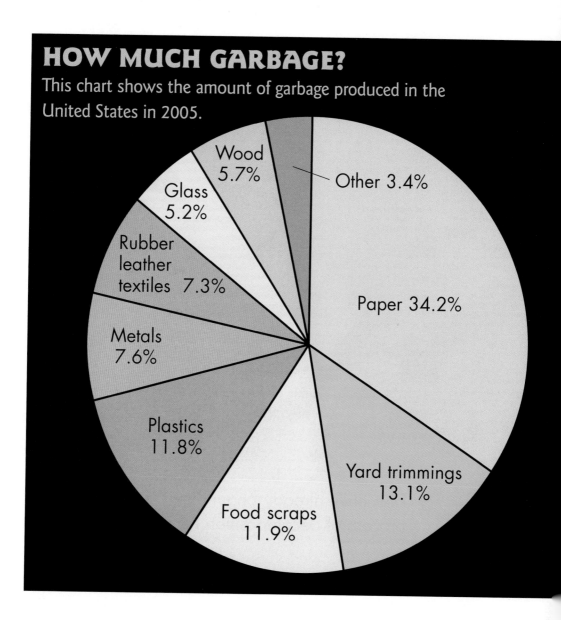

HOW MUCH GARBAGE?

This chart shows the amount of garbage produced in the United States in 2005.

- Wood 5.7%
- Glass 5.2%
- Rubber leather textiles 7.3%
- Metals 7.6%
- Plastics 11.8%
- Other 3.4%
- Paper 34.2%
- Yard trimmings 13.1%
- Food scraps 11.9%

Some waste can be poisonous. This is called **hazardous** waste. It needs to be disposed of with care.

Lots of Garbage

At school, at home, and at work, we all use lots of things. We eat many types of food. The more we use, the more garbage we create. Scientists predict that over the next few years, each American will continue to create about 4.5 pounds of trash—every day! New York City creates enough garbage each day to fill the Empire State Building.

Flies have already begun the process of decomposition here.

What Rots?

What is the difference between natural, organic material and human-made material? Take a potato and a plastic bag, for example. The potato rots quickly. The plastic bag takes hundreds of years.

ROTTING TIME

Orange peel: 6 months
Piece of paper: 2–5 months
Plastic bag: 500 years

To Rot or Not?

Leaves from trees or banana skins are natural, organic materials. They are **biodegradable**. This means that in time they will rot. Nature's own recycling team helps speed up the process. Human-made objects, such as computers, are made from manufactured materials. Some take a very long time to break down. Others will not decompose. When a computer stops working, then, how do we get rid of it?

Made to Last

Many things we use today are meant to last. They are made from materials that are hard to break down. For instance, it is important that materials such as concrete last for a long time—otherwise houses would crumble.

Computers contain some **toxic** materials. Dumping them is dangerous, so now companies can recycle them. They break up the computers and make them into new ones.

13

What Happens to Garbage?

A garbage crew takes away your trash. Much of the garbage is taken to a landfill site. This is a huge hole in the ground. There, bulldozers flatten piles of garbage. Eventually the squashed garbage is covered with layers of soil.

Landfill sites have problems. For example:
- They attract rats and other disease-carrying animals
- They smell bad
- Rotting waste releases a gas that can cause explosions
- The poison from some of the rotting garbage seeps into the ground or nearby rivers

Most of the trash in trash cans ends up in huge piles on landfill sites.

WHAT HAPPENS TO OUR TRASH?

This chart shows what happens to the garbage produced in the United States.

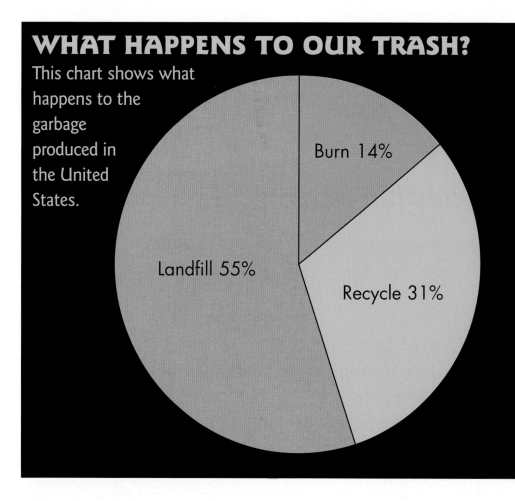

Burn 14%

Landfill 55%

Recycle 31%

Other Garbage Dangers

Some garbage is burned in large **incinerators**. However, burning garbage can release poisonous gases into the air. Dumping waste in the sea releases poisons into the water.

And there is the danger of garbage in the environment. For example, a plastic bag floating in a river looks ugly, but it can also be deadly. Wildlife can get tangled in a plastic bag. If litter is left around, animals may eat it, and this can kill them.

Garbage Solutions and Ideas

Kitchen and garden waste can be used to make healthy soil. See pages 28-29. Some garbage goes in special bins and is recycled. Find out more on page 32.

CHAPTER THREE
THE DECOMPOSERS

A vulture might feed on a dead zebra. A cockroach might feast on scraps of meat. Animals that eat the flesh of dead animals are called **scavengers**. Scavengers eat away large parts of the animals body. Then other decomposers get to work.

Cockroaches love waste. In the wild, they are important decomposers, eating away at any plant or animal remains they can find.

THE SCAVENGER HYENA

The hyena is a well-equipped scavenger. Its sharp sense of smell helps it find carcasses. Then with its sharp teeth, the hyena crunches bones. Finally, the hyena has special acids in its stomach. These acids help it digest hard bones.

Tidying Up

Vultures help keep streets clean. In some parts of the world, people do not eat beef. Here, vultures gobble up the bodies of cows that have been left lying around. This helps make sure that disease carrying animals such as rats stay away.

Scavengers are at work in the ocean, too. Sharks patrol the ocean looking for dead fish to feed on. Fish called remoras attach themselves to other sea creatures, such as sharks. From this position, they eat up what the shark leaves.

Farmers and gardeners often consider slugs as pests. Slugs eat plants and seeds but they do an important job breaking down organic matter.

Tiny Decomposers

Flies, slugs, beetles, ants, and worms are very important decomposers. Many tiny decomposers live in damp, dark places such as a pile of slushy leaves surrounded by plenty of dead material!

These small creatures chew up bits of leaves, dead animals, or dead wood. Some leave droppings that provide food for other decomposers.

WRIGGLY WORMS

Soil needs moisture, air, and nutrients to be healthy. Worms can help. First, they keep the soil healthy by loosening it and adding air as they tunnel. Then, they eat organic matter. This makes their waste, called castings, packed with nutrients. All of this will soak back into the soil.

Burying Beetles

The American burying beetle buries dead animals and then eats them. A male and female bury a dead animal, such as a mouse. Then they strip away the animal's fur or coat. The female then digs a tunnel near the rotting body and lays her eggs. When her eggs hatch, the young burying beetles have food. They will eat the rest of the dead body!

This American burying beetle helps clean up dead bodies. However, these insects are now an endangered species because there are so few of them.

Bacteria are only visible through a microscope. They may be shaped like balls, rods, or spirals.

After the larger scavengers finish, smaller creatures take over. These decomposers are called **fungi** and **bacteria**. They also eat organic matter. They release chemicals that break down matter and release its nutrients. Some nutrients, such as nitrogen and magnesium, provide energy for the decomposers. Some of them soak back into the

FUNGI IN THE SOIL
One spoonful of healthy garden soil contains about a million fungi and millions of bacteria.

soil. This provides food for growing plants. Some, such as carbon, are released into the atmosphere.

Bacteria

Bacteria are tiny **organisms** made of only one cell. They are too small to be seen with the naked eye. In fact, 20,000 bacteria laid end to end would measure less than one inch.

Fungi

Fungi are another type of organism. They were originally thought to be plants. But unlike plants, they cannot turn sunlight into food. They must eat other organisms for their food.

Fungi are tiny threadlike structures that look like spaghetti. They spread through wood or soil. Sometimes they produce bodies that we can see, such as mushrooms and toadstools.

There are over 100,000 species of fungi.

CHAPTER FOUR

FOOD FOR DECOMPOSERS

If you see a rotten log in the park, look close. It may be dead, but it may also be teeming with life. Decaying logs or even fallen trees make excellent **habitats** for mammals, birds, and even fish (if the log or tree falls in the water). As the dead tree breaks into pieces, its nutrients soak back into the soil. This creates healthy soil that will help new trees grow.

An army of decomposers work day and night. They clear the forest of fallen leaves, dead wood, and dead animals.

Woody Home

Fallen trees or dead wood provide homes to many animals. Hawks perch high above in lofty leafless perches. From there, they keep a beady eye out for anything that moves. Farther down, the hollows of dead or diseased trees make great nesting spots for owls, squirrels, and other small animals. And, down below, rotting trunks or logs make great homes for smaller animals, like frogs.

Rotting wood is a good source of food, too. Insects and small creatures such as slugs and snails will feed on it. Soon birds will be pecking at the wood, feeding on the insects inside. Fungi and bacteria eat their droppings. Before long, the wood will crumble away.

A hollow, dead tree is a perfect hideaway for this young raccoon.

Dung!

Many decomposers eat waste matter, called dung, made by other animals. For example, the dung fly lives and breeds in cow dung. Animal dung is actually full of goodness. Even decomposers' waste matter rots into the soil.

2. A cow makes waste (called dung or manure).

1. A cow eats grass.

3. The nutrients in the manure make the grass grow well.

Manure Enriches the Soil

Soil is a mixture of tiny bits of rock and natural waste. Farmers sometimes add waste from their animals, called manure, to the soil. Manure is packed with nutrients that enrich the soil. A soil rich in nutrients helps the growth of healthy crops.

This dung beetle rolls a large ball of dung. It buries the ball and then lays eggs in it. When the eggs hatch, the young beetles eat the dung.

Cows make a lot of manure! In Australia, cows were making about 331,000 tons (300,000 tonnes) of cow dung every day. This attracted thousands of flies. Finally, scientists introduced the dung beetle to the country. The beetles ate away mounds of manure.

MANURE AS FUEL

Pig manure can be turned into oil! To do this, the smelly waste is heated to high temperatures. This turns it into a liquid that can be used as a fuel.

This cheese is moldy, but it is perfectly safe to eat. The blue marks are mold, grown from a fungus. But watch out, many fungi are poisonous.

Fresh food does not last. If you leave a pear for too long, it goes soft. Soon **mold** may grow.

Mold

Mold is a type of fungus. It can be white, blue, green, yellow, pink, red, or black. Most molds that grow on foods

WHAT A STINKER!

The rafflesia plant stinks like rotting flesh! This smell attracts flies. They land in the huge plant. When they fly on, they help spread the plant's seeds.

such as bread, cheese, fruit, and vegetables can contain poisons. Some blue veined cheeses are made with a mold that is safe to eat.

Keeping Healthy

You can often smell rotten food or see that it is "spoiled." Decaying food changes color and can smell unpleasant. It is important not to eat food that has spoiled. It can make you sick.

If you are sick, the doctor may give you medicine to make you better. Some medicines are made from molds. These molds kill off the bacteria that are making you sick.

Medicines such as penicillin and other antibiotics are made from fungi. They attack the unfriendly bacteria that cause illness.

In a Compost Bin

Instead of throwing apple cores or carrot tops into the trash, throw them in a **compost** bin. Composting is a way of reusing garden or kitchen waste. In a compost bin, the waste decomposes quickly, and nutrients go back into the soil.

Scraps of uncooked food soon decompose in a compost bin. This makes a rich, moist soil to help new plants grow.

DECOMPOSITION

In order to decompose quickly, potato peelings need:

- Moisture
- Oxygen
- Warmth
- A few decomposers such as slugs and beetles

LOTS OF BANANA SKINS

One person throws away 428 pounds (194 kilograms) of natural waste each year. That's as much as 2,800 banana skins.

When you throw an apple core into a compost bin…
1. Tiny organisms eat away at the apple core.
2. This creates heat and encourages other decomposers to grow.
3. As the compost cools down, fungi starts to work.
4. In about nine months, the apple core has disappeared.
5. Nutrients from the core have soaked back into the soil.
6. New plants will use these nutrients to grow.

The process of decomposition provides life for young plants. As nutrients from dead plants soak into the soil, new plants take them up.

You can see that rot and decay help keep nature in balance, but they can also cause damage.

House Rot

Mold can grow inside damp houses. This kind of mold can ruin carpets and furniture. Another harmful growth is dry rot. Dry rot eats away at wood until it crumbles.

Unhealthy Germs

Some bacteria are friendly. Friendly ones are found in foods such as yogurt. We also have plenty of friendly bacteria living in our bodies. But not all bacteria are friendly. Unfriendly bacteria are sometimes called germs. They can cause sickness in humans. That is why you must wash your hands after touching the soil.

The Good and Bad

Some fungi are poisonous. They can kill living trees. They are also a main cause of crop destruction. Some fungi attack certain crops of potatoes. During the nineteenth century, a fungus, known as potato blight, destroyed the main Irish crop. This led to a terrible shortage of food. Many people starved.

(Opposite) Friendly bacteria live in some yogurts. They help keep you healthy by fighting unfriendly bacteria that cause ill health.

CHAPTER FIVE

RECYCLE

Nature is busy recycling natural waste. But we need to help out with the garbage people create. First, we need to deal with the material that is thrown away as garbage. Second, we need to cut down on the amount of garbage we create. To stop garbage from swamping our planet, we must reduce, reuse, and recycle.

THE 3 Rs

Reduce
Use fewer things! Avoid buying products covered in unnecessary packaging.

Reuse
Reuse things instead of buying new ones. Reuse items such as plastic bags.

Recycle
Items made of metal, glass, plastic, and paper can be turned into new

ROTTING PLASTIC

Scientists keep looking for ways to help nature in its recycling. For example, adding certain materials, including corn starch, to plastic bags helps them decompose more quickly. Some plastics are made with materials that degrade in strong sunlight.

Dung Power

Natural waste can be reused. Dung, for example, can be turned into a fuel. When living things rot, they produce gases. One of these gases is methane. It is also found in animal waste. The waste is put in a special tank that collects the gas. Then the gas is used as a fuel for cooking and heating.

Gas made from organic matter is called biogas. The biogas made in this biogas plant in Sweden is used as a fuel to power trains.

Why Recycle?

Plastic, glass, and metal are made from raw materials that come from the ground. Plastic is made from oil. Glass is made from sand. Metal is taken from rocks. One day these materials will run out. They cannot be replaced. They are called nonrenewable materials. A can made of steel can be recycled several times. It can even be made into new objects such as a bicycle.

Using Energy

Coal, natural gas, and oil are fuels that come from raw materials. We burn these fuels to make electricity. This provides the power needed to make objects such as tin cans.

WHAT CAN WE RECYCLE?

This bench is made from recycled plastic bags!

Metals, such as nickel, occur naturally in the Earth but they take millions of years to form. We are using them up more quickly than they will be replaced. This is why it is important to reuse and recycle—otherwise we will run out of these precious resources.

At this mine they are extracting nickel. Recycling metals like nickel helps save these nonrenewable materials.

Waste and Need

People buy, use, and dispose of products at a rapid rate. Products made of human-made materials are a problem. Think about items such as mobile phones, computers, and refrigerators. All of these things make garbage when they are no longer of use. This is why it is important to recycle as many things as possible.

What's Recycled?

Today, more people than ever are recycling manufactured objects. They want to protect the natural balance of planet Earth.

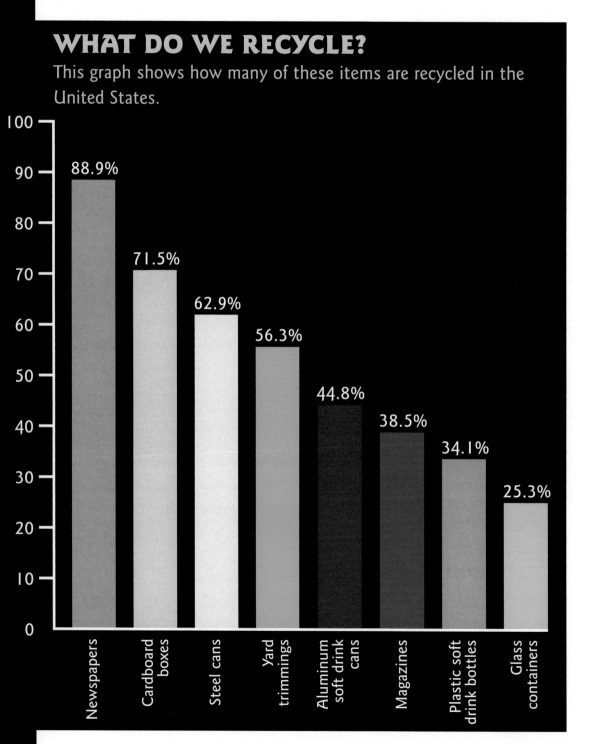

WHAT DO WE RECYCLE?

This graph shows how many of these items are recycled in the United States.

- Newspapers: 88.9%
- Cardboard boxes: 71.5%
- Steel cans: 62.9%
- Yard trimmings: 56.3%
- Aluminum soft drink cans: 44.8%
- Magazines: 38.5%
- Plastic soft drink bottles: 34.1%
- Glass containers: 25.3%

RECYCLING FACTS

- Every day American businesses use enough paper to circle Earth 20 times! But recycling just one ton of paper can save 17 trees, 380 gallons of oil, 3 cubic yards of space, 4,000 kilowatts of energy and 7,000 gallons of water!
- One recycled metal can saves enough energy to run a television for three hours.
- Some things are turned into amazing objects.

  CDs ━━━━▶ pencils

  Plastic bags ━━━━▶ clothes

  Shipping containers ━━━━▶ houses

This house is built from shipping containers. It is a great example of recycling.

Dangerous Garbage

What can we do with poisonous or dangerous waste? Burying it lets poisons seep underground. Burning it releases poisons into the air. There are many hazardous wastes that we do not know how to get rid of.

In the United States, over 36,000 hazardous waste sites exist. These store used oil, battery acid, heavy metals, cleaning fluids, pesticides, old paint, plastics, and radioactive wastes.

Nuclear Waste

Some electricity is made using nuclear power. Nuclear power plants produce dangerous waste. This waste remains very harmful to people and the environment for hundreds of years. At the moment, nuclear waste is stored in underground concrete tanks.

Space Garbage

Today, space stations and satellites float high up above Earth. These things also create waste. Leftover or mislaid nuts, bolts, and gloves are flying through space at around 17,500 miles (28,164 km) per hour.

(Opposite) There is little room for junk onboard a space station such as the International Space Station. Some of the unwanted junk is chucked into space where it either burns up or hurtles around at great speed.

Rotten Stuff

There is often more to garbage than the smelly stuff in the trash can.

Packed Up

Ancient Egyptians sometimes made "mummies" out of dead bodies. They wrapped the bodies and treated them with

special acids. They also removed the heart and other organs to get rid of any moisture. Decomposers need moisture and air to break things down. Without these, the bodies did not rot.

Freezing Cold

In extremely cold conditions, fungi and bacteria do not survive. Some dead bodies have been found packed in freezing ice. The bodies have not decayed.

A mummy is a preserved body. Ancient Egyptians mummified dead bodies by drying them out after death.

Rotten Crime

Rot and decay can help solve crimes. Scientists examine a body to figure out how far the decay has spread. From this, they can then determine when the person died.

A branch of science called forensic entomology examines insects and other decomposers. This helps solve crimes by working out when a person died.

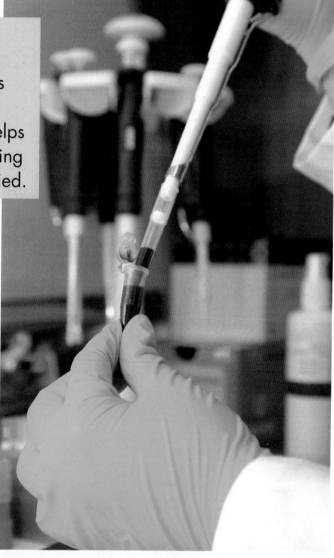

OLD GARBAGE

We learn a lot about other cultures and civilizations from what they have thrown away. Objects such as pottery or jewelry give us information about how people from past cultures lived.

It's Your World

After this book, you may never look at rot and decay the same again. Fruit rotting beneath a tree, the buzz of a fly, a decayed bit of wood—everything will remind you of the important process of decomposition. Only now you will know it's all part of a natural balance.

REMEMBER THE 3 Rs

- Recycle whatever you can.
- Reduce what you buy.
- Reuse where you can.

Compost It

Ask your parents to start a compost bin. You don't need a garden to do this. Is there a small garden at school? Make sure it is kept clear of litter. Carefully replace any logs or twigs you disturb. Remember, there is lots of life and death going on underfoot. Disturbing anything can destroy the process of rot and decay for many creatures.

JUST IMAGINE

If nature did not clear up its own waste, the Earth's surface would be covered with a thick layer of dead bodies! These Marabou storks are scavengers and feed on dead animals in Africa.

Rot and decay keep our world healthy. Rot clears dead matter and provides plenty of nutrients for new plants to grow.

GLOSSARY

bacteria (bak TIHR ee uh) — organism made of a single
cell, invisible unless seen through a microscope

biodegradable (bye oh di GRAY duh buhl) — something
that can be broken down and rot

chemical (KEM uh kuhl) — substance used in chemistry

compost (KOM pohst) — kitchen and garden waste left to
decompose

decompose (dee kuhm POSE) — when an animal or plant
breaks down into small parts and releases nutrients from
the waste

ecosystem (EE koh siss tuhm) — community of plants and
animals

environment (en VYE ruhn muhnt) — natural surroundings

food chain (food chayn) — transferring food energy from
one animal or plant to another

fungi (FUHNG gye) — organisms that live off other animals

habitat (HAB uh tat) — a place where animals or plants live

hazardous (HAZ ur duhss) — dangerous

incinerator (in SIN uh ray tur) — a large oven where waste is burned

mold (mohld) — a type of fungus

nutrient (NOO tree uhnt) — food that animals and plants need

organic matter (or GAN ik MAT ur) — natural waste that decomposes

organism (OR guh niz uhm) — any living thing

recycle (ree SYE kuhl) — to make a new object out of an old one

scavenger (SKAV uhnj ur) — an animal that eats the flesh of dead animals

toxic (TOK sik) — poisonous

FURTHER INFORMATION

Books

Carbon-Oxygen and Nitrogen Cycles: Respiration, Photosynthesis and Decomposition. Rebecca Harman. Heinemann, 2005.

Earth's Garbage Crisis (What if we do nothing?) Christine Dorion. World Almanac Library, 2007.

Food Chains And Webs. (Life Processes/2nd Edition). Holly Wallace. Heinemann, 2006.

Recycling. Jen Green. Stargazer Books, 2006.

Websites to visit

http://www.metrokc.gov/dnr/kidsweb/index.htm
King County (Washington State) website about natural resources. Information, games, and quizzes on water, wildlife, recycling, and hazardous waste.

http://www.countrysideinfo.co.uk/decompos.htm
Information on decomposition, including images showing the stages of decay in a dead rabbit.

http://www.eia.doe.gov/kids/energyfacts/saving/
recycling/solidwaste/primer.html
Information on garbage and saving energy, as well as lots of activities and games.

http://www.astc.org/exhibitions/rotten/nature.htm
Information about how nature deals with waste.

www.recyclenow.com/home_composting/composting/
what_happens_in.html
A site that shows you what happens to the waste in a compost bin.

INDEX